Ninja Dual Zone Air Fryer Cookbook UK 2023

1200 Days Fast and Healthy Family-Favourites Ninja Air Fryer Crispy Recipes That Will Love Everyone

By Margo Robinson

© Copyright 2023 All rights reserved

This report is towards furnishing precise and solid data concerning the point and issue secured. The production is sold with the possibility that the distributor isn't required to render bookkeeping, formally allowed, or something else, qualified administrations. On the off chance that exhortation is important, lawful, or proficient, a rehearsed individual in the calling ought to be requested.

The Declaration of Principles, which was also recognized and endorsed by the Committee of the American Bar Association and the Committee of Publishers and Associations. Not the slightest bit is it lawful to replicate, copy, or transmit any piece of this report in either electronic methods or the printed group. Recording of this distribution is carefully disallowed, and any capacity of this report isn't permitted except if with composed authorization from the distributor. All rights held.

The data given in this is expressed, to be honest, and predictable, in that any risk, as far as absentmindedness or something else, by any utilization or maltreatment of any approaches, procedures, or bearings contained inside is the singular and articulate obligation of the beneficiary peruser. By no means will any lawful obligation or fault be held against the distributor for any reparation, harm, or money-related misfortune because of the data in this, either straightforwardly or by implication.

Particular creators claim all copyrights not held by the distributor.

The data in this is offered for educational purposes exclusively and is all-inclusive as so. The introduction of the data is without a contract or any sort of assurance confirmation. The trademarks that are utilized are with no assent, and the distribution of the trademark is without consent or support by the trademark proprietor. All trademarks and brands inside this book are for explaining purposes just and are simply possessed by the proprietors, not partnered with this record.

Contents

INTRODUCTION 8

The Ninja Dual Zone Air Fryer Is Here To Rule Your Kitchen! 8

The Amazing Features 9

Why You Should Buy Ninja Dual Zone Air Fryer Today! 10

BREAKFAST RECIPES 13

RASPBERRY ROLLS 14

BREAKFAST PEA TORTILLA 15

CINNAMON AND CREAM CHEESE OATS 16

POTATO AND LEEK FRITTATA 17

ESPRESSO OATMEAL 18

CHERRIES RISOTTO 19

WALNUTS AND PEAR OATMEAL 20

ALMONDS & RAISINS PUDDING 21

MUSHROOM OATMEAL 22

DATES AND MILLET PUDDING 23

LUNCH RECIPES	24
EASY CHICKEN LUNCH	25
CHICKEN AND CORN CASSEROLE	26
MUSHROOM CHEESE LUNCH	27
CHICKEN AND ZUCCHINI MIX	28
HASSELBACK POTATOES	29
CHICKEN & QUINOA CASSEROLE	30
SWEET CHILI POTATO WEDGES	31
BRUSSELS SPROUTS LUNCH	32
GREEN BEANS LUNCH	33
CREAMY AIR FRIED POTATO WITH BACON STRIPS	34
ROASTED PUMPKIN	35
PARMESAN MUSHROOMS	36
STUFFED EGGPLANT LUNCH	37
PORK SAUSAGE WITH RICE	38
CAULIFLOWER CAKES	39
MUSHROOMS WITH BACON AND SOUR CREAM	40

CREAMY BRUSSELS SPROUTS 41

BARLEY RISOTTO 42

CAULIFLOWER RICE WITH MUSHROOMS 43

BEER RISOTTO 44

DINNER RECIPES 45

THYME AND PARSLEY SALMON 46

EASY DUCK BREASTS 47

GARLIC AND BELL PEPPER BEEF 48

SPINACH PIE 49

TROUT WITH BUTTER SAUCE 50

DUCK BREASTS WITH ENDIVES 51

MARINATED LAMB AND VEGGIES 52

BALSAMIC ARTICHOKES 53

CREAMY SALMON 54

CHICKEN BREASTS WITH TOMATOES SAUCE 55

CREAMY LAMB 56

CHEESY ARTICHOKES 57

ITALIAN BARRAMUNDI FILLETS AND TOMATO SALSA 58

CHICKEN AND ASPARAGUS 59

LAMB SHANKS 60

BEET SALAD AND PARSLEY DRESSING... 61

SALMON WITH AVOCADO SALSA 62

CHICKEN THIGHS AND APPLE MIX 63

LAMB ROAST WITH POTATOES 64

ARTICHOKES AND SPECIAL SAUCE 65

SNACKS RECIPES 66

WRAPPED SHRIMP... 67

BROCCOLI PATTIES 68

MEAT & CHEESE STUFFED PEPPERS 69

CHEESY ZUCCHINI SNACK 70

SPINACH BALLS.. 71

MAYO MUSHROOMS SNACK.. 72

CHEESY PARTY WINGS 73

SWEET BACON SNACK 74

CHEESE STICKS 75

BLUE CHEESE CHICKEN ROLLS 76

DESSERT RECIPES 77

LEMON BARS 78

PEARS WITH ESPRESSO CREAM 79

FIGS AND COCONUT BUTTER MIX 80

POPPYSEED CAKE 81

SWEET SQUARES 82

PLUM BARS 83

ORANGE COOKIES 84

PLUM AND CURRANT TART 86

CASHEW BARS 88

BROWN BUTTER COOKIES 89

INTRODUCTION

The Ninja Dual Zone Air Fryer Is Here To Rule Your Kitchen!

This appliance has a striking design with two roomy drawers, removable non-stick crisper plates, and a matte black exterior accentuated with superior shiny stainless steel. You will undoubtedly be impressed by the construction and adaptability of the Ninja Dual air fryer.

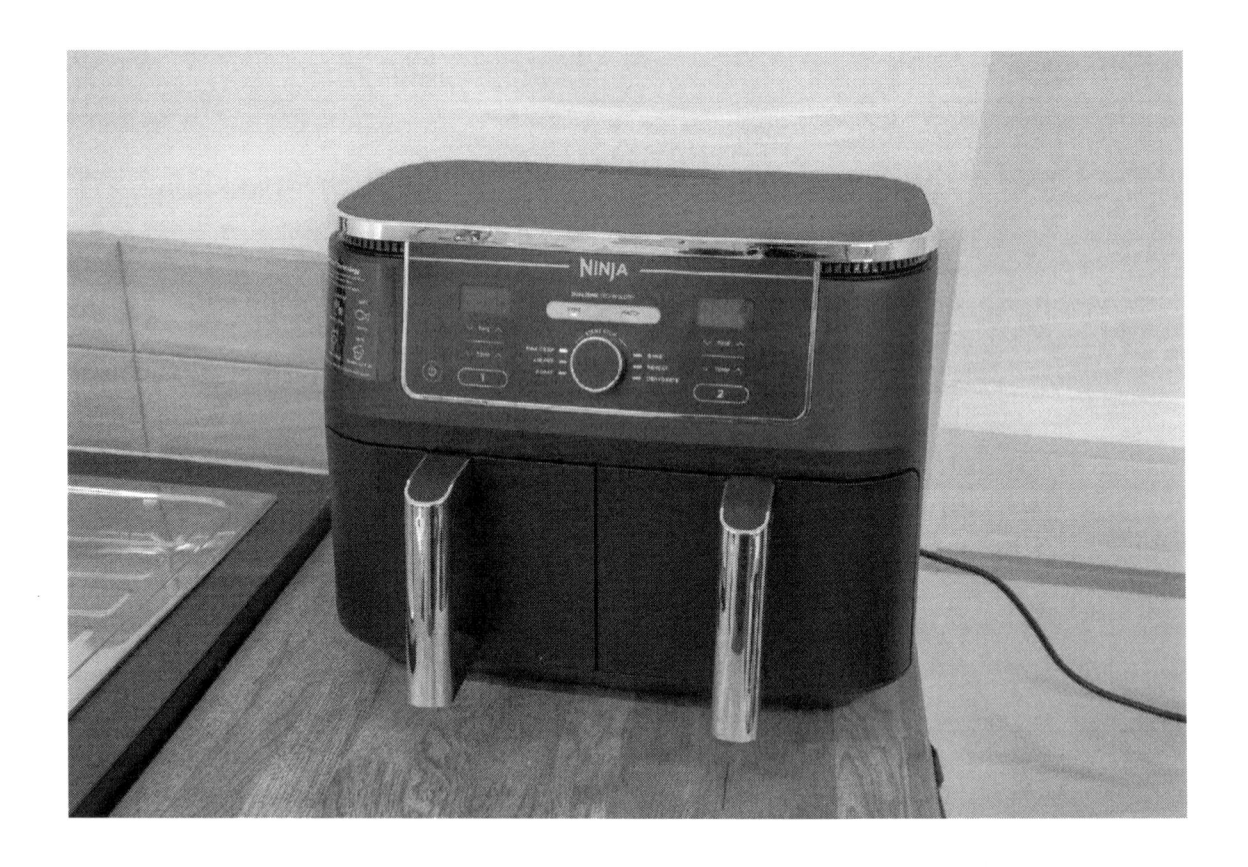

It can roast, bake, reheat, and cook food from frozen to crispy in a matter of minutes in addition to dehydrating fruits and vegetables. As an air fryer, it is easy to use. Additionally, Ninja claims that it consumes 75% less energy than a typical oven.

When it comes to cooking, timing is essential. The Ninja Food Dual Zone Air Fryer makes the timing and duration decisions. You can change the temperatures, timings, and cooking programs for both drawers by using different cooking zones.

The Amazing Features

• TWO SEPARATE BASKETS: The original air fryer, the XL air fryer eliminates back-to-back cooking like a traditional single-basket air fryer by enabling you to prepare two different meals at once.

• SMART FINISH & MATCH COOK: DualZone Technology offers you the choice of the Smart Finish function, which allows you to cook two items in two different ways that finish at the same time, or the Match Cook button, which makes it simple to replicate settings between zones to use the entire 8-qt capacity.

• 6-IN-1 FUNCTIONALITY OPERATIONS: Includes six flexible cooking modes, including air fry, air broil, roast, bake, reheat, and dehydrate.

• Extra-Large (XL) CAPACITY: The 8-quart air fryer's capacity can accommodate up to 2 kilograms of chicken wings or French fries for convenient family meals.

• DIFFERENT HEATING ZONES: Each of the two distinct, 4 quart zones has a rapid heater, cyclonic fan, and cooking basket.

• EASY CLEANING: Crisper plates that can go in the dishwasher and easily sanitized baskets.

• LESS FAT: Using conventional air frying methods may result in up to 75% more fat. Deep-fried, hand-cut French fries were put to the test.

• WIDE TEMPERATURE RANGE: 40°C to 230°F enables you to gently remove moisture from food while gently cooking and crisping food with convection heat.

Why You Should Buy Ninja Dual Zone Air Fryer Today!

The air fryer that simultaneously cooks two different dishes in two different ways. Additional to an air fryer. There are six different ways to cook: air fry, max crisp, roast, bake, and reheat. Timing is everything when it comes to cooking. The Ninja Dual Zone 7.6 litre air fryer automates the planning and scheduling for you with 2 separate cooking zones.

You can simultaneously prepare two separate dishes and have them both ready to eat at the same time! Synchronization: Both zones are prepared to serve at the same time despite the diverse foods, occasions, and programs. Want to air fry in one area and roast in another? No issue! Do chicken wings and fries require different cooking times? There is no need to use multiple appliances or let your side sit out to cool while your main cooks because both drawers will be done cooking at the same time, allowing you to enjoy freshly prepared mains and sides together. Preparing food for additional visitors versus serving the entire family?

Cook twice as much food in the same amount of time by using the same cooking program and timing in both drawers. Just preparing food for oneself? Cooking is possible in a single drawer, no issue.

Cook dishes that the entire family will enjoy in under half the time it takes to use a fan oven—up to 75% faster. Suitable when you need to quickly set the table for dinner. (Tested including preheating against sausages and fish fingers.) Air fry, max crisp, roast, bake, reheat, and dehydrate are six different cooking methods.

BREAKFAST RECIPES

Raspberry Rolls

Prep Time: 30-32 Min | Cook Time: 20-21 Min | Serves: 6

Calories: 260 | Fat: 5.2g | Carbs: 8.9g | Protein: 6.1g

INGREDIENTS

- 250ml milk
- 4 tbsp butter
- 650g flour
- 2 tsp yeast
- 50g sugar
- 1 egg

For the filling:

- 30ml cream cheese, soft
- 350g raspberries
- 1 tsp vanilla extract
- 5 tbsp sugar
- 1 tbsp cornstarch
- Zest from 1 lemon, grated

DIRECTIONS

1. Take a mixing bowl and combine flour, sugar, and yeast. Stir until well combined.
2. Add milk and egg to the mixture and stir until a dough forms. Set the dough aside to rise for 30-32 Minutes. Once it has risen, transfer the dough to a working surface and roll it out until it is smooth.
3. In a separate bowl, mix together cream cheese, sugar, vanilla, and lemon zest until well combined. Pour this mixture over the dough that has been rolled out.
4. In another bowl, mix raspberries with cornstarch. Stir until the raspberries are well coated. Spread the raspberry mixture over the cream cheese mixture on the dough.
5. Roll up the dough and cut it into medium-sized pieces. Place the pieces in your air fryer and spray them with cooking spray. Cook at 175°C for 30-32 Minutes.
6. Serve the rolls for breakfast.

Breakfast Pea Tortilla

Prep Time: 10-11 Min | Cook Time: 7 Min | Serves: 6

Calories: 190 | Fat: 5.1g | Carbs: 8.2g | Protein: 7.1g

INGREDIENTS

- 250g baby peas
- 4 tbsp butter
- 350g yogurt
- 8 eggs
- 100g mint, chopped
- Salt & black pepper

DIRECTIONS

1. Begin by melting butter in a pan over medium heat. Once the butter is melted, add peas and stir. Cook for a few minutes until the peas are heated through.
2. In a separate bowl, mix together half of the yogurt with salt, pepper, eggs, and mint. Whisk until well combined.
3. Pour the yogurt mixture over the peas in the pan and toss to combine. Transfer the mixture to your air fryer and cook at 175°C for 7 minutes.
4. Spread the remaining yogurt over your tortilla, slice it, and serve.

Cinnamon and Cream Cheese Oats

Prep Time: 10-11 Min | Cook Time: 25-26 Min | Serves: 4

Calories: 149 | Fat: 6.2g | Carbs: 24.9g | Protein: 7.1g

INGREDIENTS

- 200g steel oats
- 700ml milk
- 1 tbsp butter
- 150g raisins
- 1 tsp cinnamon powder
- 50g brown sugar
- 2 tbsp white sugar
- 60ml cream cheese

DIRECTIONS

1. Melt the butter in a skillet that fits your air fryer over medium heat. Add the oats and toss for 3 minutes to toast them.

2. Pour milk and raisins into the air fryer, stir, and cook for 20-21 Minutes at 175°C.

3. In the meantime, combine cinnamon and brown sugar in a bowl and stir.

4. Whisk together cream cheese and white sugar in a separate bowl.

5. Distribute the oats into bowls and sprinkle cream cheese and cinnamon over each one.

Potato and Leek Frittata

Prep Time: 10-11 Min | Cook Time: 18 Min | Serves: 4

Calories: 270 | Fat: 6.2g | Carbs: 11.9g | Protein: 6.1g

INGREDIENTS

- 2 gold potatoes, boiled, peeled and chopped
- 2 tbsp butter
- 2 leeks, sliced
- Salt & black pepper
- 60ml whole milk
- 10 eggs, whisked
- 150g fromage blanc, crumbled

DIRECTIONS

1. To start, heat a pan over medium heat and melt the butter. Once the butter is melted, add leeks and stir. Cook for 4 minutes until the leeks are softened.
2. Add potatoes, salt, pepper, eggs, cheese, and milk to the pan. Whisk everything together until well combined. Cook for an additional 1 minute.
3. Transfer the mixture to your air fryer and cook at 175°C for 13 minutes.
4. Slice the frittata and divide it among plates to serve.

Espresso Oatmeal

Prep Time: 10-11 Min | Cook Time: 17 Min | Serves: 4

Calories: 258 | Fat: 7.2g | Carbs: 37.9g | Protein: 6.1g

INGREDIENTS

- 250ml milk
- 200g steel cut oats
- 600ml water
- 2 tbsp sugar
- 1 tsp espresso powder
- 2 tsp vanilla extract

DIRECTIONS

1. Combine the oats with the milk, sugar, and espresso powder in a pan that will fit your air fryer, stir, and cook for 17 minutes at 180°C.

2. Stir in the vanilla essence and add the remaining ingredients. After 5 minutes, divide the mixture into dishes and serve as breakfast.

Cherries Risotto

Prep Time: 10-11 Min | Cook Time: 12-13 Min | Serves: 4

Calories: 158 | Fat: 12.1g | Carbs: 22.9g | Protein: 8.1g

INGREDIENTS

- 300g Arborio rice
- 1 and ½ tsp cinnamon powder
- 65g brown sugar
- A pinch of salt
- 2 tbsp butter
- 2 apples, cored and sliced
- 250ml apple juice
- 700ml milk
- 100g cherries, dried

DIRECTIONS

1. Melt the butter in a pan that fits your air fryer. Add the rice, stir, and cook for 4-5 minutes.

2. To your air fryer, add the sugar, apples, apple juice, milk, cinnamon, and cherries. Stir. Cook for 8 minutes at 175°C.

3. Dish out for breakfast after dividing into bowls.

Walnuts and Pear Oatmeal

Prep Time: 5 Min | Cook Time: 12-13 Min | Serves: 4

Calories: 228 | Fat: 6.2g | Carbs: 20.9g | Protein: 5.1g

INGREDIENTS

- 250ml water
- 1 tbsp butter, soft
- 50g brown sugar
- ½ tsp cinnamon powder
- 200g rolled oats
- 100g walnuts, chopped
- 400g pear, peeled and chopped
- 100g raisins

DIRECTIONS

1. Combine milk with sugar, butter, oats, cinnamon, raisins, pears, and walnuts in a heat-resistant dish that will fit your air fryer. Stir. Add mixture to fryer. Cook at 180°C for 12-13 Minutes.

2. Dish out after dividing into bowls. Serve and enjoy!

Almonds & Raisins Pudding

Prep Time: 5 Min | Cook Time: 8 Min | Serves: 4

Calories: 253 | Fat: 6.1g | Carbs: 38.9g | Protein: 12.1g

INGREDIENTS

- 200g brown rice
- 100g coconut chips
- 250ml milk
- 500ml water
- 125ml maple syrup
- 50g raisins
- 50g almonds
- A pinch of cinnamon powder

DIRECTIONS

1. Place the rice, water, and heat source in a pan that will fit your air fryer. Cook the rice until it is tender and drain.

2. In your air fryer, combine the milk, coconut chips, almonds, raisins, cinnamon, and maple syrup. Stir well. Cook for 8 minutes at 180°C.

3. Dish up the rice pudding into bowls.

Mushroom Oatmeal

Prep Time: 10-11 Min | Cook Time: 20-21 Min | Serves: 4

Calories: 280 | Fat: 8.2g | Carbs: 19.9g | Protein: 17.1g

INGREDIENTS

- 1 small yellow onion, chopped
- 200g steel cut oats
- 2 garlic cloves, minced
- 2 tbsp butter
- 125ml water
- 300ml canned chicken stock
- 3 thyme springs, chopped
- 2 tbsp extra virgin olive oil
- 100g gouda cheese, grated
- 225g mushroom, sliced
- Salt & black pepper

DIRECTIONS

1. Melt the butter in a skillet that is large enough to hold your air fryer. Add the onions and garlic, stir, and cook for 4 minutes.

2. Stir together the oats, water, salt, pepper, stock, and thyme before adding them to your air fryer. Cook for 16 minutes at 180°C.

3. In the meantime, prepare the breakfast by heating a skillet with the olive oil over medium heat, adding the mushrooms, cooking them for 3 minutes, then adding the cheese and oats and stirring.

Dates and Millet Pudding

Prep Time: 10-11 Min | Cook Time: 15-16 Min | Serves: 4

Calories: 235 | Fat: 6.1g | Carbs: 17.9g | Protein: 6.4g

INGREDIENTS

- 100ml milk
- 200ml water
- 150g millet
- 4 dates, pitted
- Honey for serving

DIRECTIONS

1. Place the millet in a pan that will fit your air fryer. Add the dates, milk, and water. Stir. Place the pan in your air fryer. Cook for 15-16 Minutes at 180°C.

2. Distribute amongst plates, top with honey, and serve as breakfast.

LUNCH RECIPES

Easy Chicken Lunch

Prep Time: 10-11 Min | Cook Time: 20-21 Min | Serves: 6

Calories: 175 | Fat: 7.1g | Carbs: 10.2g | Protein: 4.9g

INGREDIENTS

- 1 bunch kale, chopped
- Salt & black pepper
- 60ml chicken stock
- 200g chicken, shredded
- 3 carrots, chopped
- 200g shiitake mushrooms, roughly sliced

DIRECTIONS

1. Toss stock and kale in a blender, give it a few pulses, and then transfer the mixture into an air fryer-compatible pan.

2. In an air fryer, combine the chicken, mushrooms, and carrots. Season with salt and pepper to taste, mix, and cook for 18 minutes at 175°C.

Chicken and Corn Casserole

Prep Time: 10-11 Min | Cook Time: 30-32 Min | Serves: 6

Calories: 341 | Fat: 12.1g | Carbs: 20.2g | Protein: 42.9g

INGREDIENTS

- 250ml chicken stock
- 2 tsp garlic powder
- Salt & black pepper
- 175ml canned coconut milk
- 300g green lentils
- 1 kg chicken breasts, skinless, boneless and cubed
- 70g cilantro, chopped
- 500g corn
- 3 handfuls spinach
- 3 green onions, chopped

DIRECTIONS

1. Combine stock, coconut milk, salt, pepper, garlic powder, chicken, and lentils in a pan that fits your air fryer.

2. Incorporate spinach, corn, green onions, and cilantro in your air fryer and cook for 30-32 Minutes at 175°C.

Mushroom Cheese Lunch

Prep Time: 10-11 Min | Cook Time: 25-26 Min | Serves: 4

Calories: 169 | Fat: 8.2g | Carbs: 18.2g | Protein: 6.8g

INGREDIENTS

- 10 button mushrooms, stems removed
- 1 tbsp Italian seasoning
- Salt & black pepper
- 2 tbsp cheddar cheese, grated
- 1 tbsp olive oil
- 2 tbsp mozzarella, grated
- 1 tbsp dill, chopped

DIRECTIONS

1. Combine mushrooms with Italian seasoning, salt, pepper, oil, and dill in a bowl and toss to combine.

2. Arrange mushrooms in the basket of your air fryer, top with mozzarella and cheddar, and cook for 8 minutes at 180°C.

3. Serve and enjoy!

Chicken and Zucchini Mix

Prep Time: 10-11 Min | Cook Time: 20-21 Min | Serves: 4

Calories: 342 | Fat: 8.2g | Carbs: 12.2g | Protein: 16.3g

INGREDIENTS

- 4 zucchinis, cut with a spiralizer
- ½ kg chicken breasts, skinless, boneless and cubed
- 2 garlic cloves, minced
- 1 tsp olive oil
- Salt & black pepper
- 300g cherry tomatoes, halved
- 100g almonds, chopped

For the pesto:

- 300g basil
- 300g kale, chopped
- 1 tbsp lemon juice
- 1 garlic clove
- 150g pine nuts
- 125ml olive oil
- A pinch of salt

DIRECTIONS

1. Combine basil with kale, lemon juice, garlic, pine nuts, oil, and a pinch of salt in a food processor. Blend thoroughly in the processor, then set aside.

2. Heat the oil in the pan that is designed to suit your air fryer over medium heat. Add the garlic, swirl, and cook for 1 minute.

3. Gently toss in the chicken, salt, pepper, almonds, zucchini noodles, garlic, cherry tomatoes, and the pesto you created earlier. Place in the preheated air fryer, and cook for 17 minutes at 180°C.

4. Distribute among serving plates and enjoy.

Hasselback Potatoes

Prep Time: 10-11 Min | Cook Time: 20-21 Min | Serves: 2

Calories: 170 | Fat: 6.2g | Carbs: 9.2g | Protein: 6.1g

INGREDIENTS

- 2 potatoes
- 2 tbsp olive oil
- 1 tsp garlic, minced
- Salt & black pepper
- ½ tsp oregano, dried
- ½ tsp basil, dried
- ½ tsp sweet paprika

DIRECTIONS

1. Peel and thinly slice the potatoes. Whisk vigorously to combine oil, garlic, salt, pepper, oregano, basil, and paprika in a bowl.

2. Apply this mixture to the potatoes, put them in the basket of your air fryer, and fry them for 20-21 Minutes at 180°C.

3. Serve and enjoy!

Chicken & Quinoa Casserole

Prep Time: 10-11 Min | Cook Time: 30-32 Min | Serves: 8

Calories: 362 | Fat: 12.1g | Carbs: 22.3g | Protein: 25.9g

INGREDIENTS

- 200g quinoa, already cooked
- ½ kg chicken breast
- 400g canned black beans
- 350g corn
- 100g cilantro, chopped
- 6 kale leaves, chopped
- 100g green onions, chopped
- 200ml tomato sauce
- 200ml salsa
- 2 tsp chili powder
- 2 tsp cumin, ground
- 600g mozzarella cheese, shredded
- 1 tbsp garlic powder
- Cooking spray
- 2 jalapeno peppers, chopped

DIRECTIONS

1. Cook and shred the chicken breast. Use cooking spray to coat a baking dish that will fit your air fryer.

2. Include the following ingredients: mozzarella, quinoa, black beans, chicken, corn, cilantro, , green onions, kale, salsa, cumin, tomato sauce, chili powder, and garlic powder.

3. Toss to combine, then cook at 175°C for 17 minutes.

4. Slice and serve meal warm.

Sweet Chili Potato Wedges

Prep Time: 10-11 Min | Cook Time: 25-26 Min | Serves: 4

Calories: 169 | Fat: 8.2g | Carbs: 18.2g | Protein: 6.8g

INGREDIENTS

- 2 potatoes
- 1 tbsp olive oil
- Salt & black pepper
- 3 tbsp sour cream
- 2 tbsp sweet chili sauce

DIRECTIONS

1. Cut potato into wedges. Toss the potato wedges in a bowl with the oil, salt, and pepper. Place them in the basket of an air fryer and cook for 25-26 Minutes at 180°C, rotating them once.

2. Arrange potato wedges on plates and top with sour cream and chili sauce.

Brussels Sprouts Lunch

Prep Time: 10-11 Min | Cook Time: 15-16 Min | Serves: 4

Calories: 169 | Fat: 6.2g | Carbs: 12.1g | Protein: 6.2g

INGREDIENTS

- ½ kg Brussels sprouts
- Salt & black pepper
- 6 tsp olive oil
- ½ tsp thyme, chopped
- 100ml mayonnaise
- 2 tbsp roasted garlic

DIRECTIONS

1. In your air fryer, combine the oil, salt, and Brussels sprouts. Toss well, and cook for 15-16 Minutes at 200°C.

2. In the meantime, whisk together the thyme, mayonnaise, and garlic in a bowl.

3. Distribute the Brussels sprouts among plates, top with garlic sauce, and serve.

Green Beans Lunch

Prep Time: 10-11 Min | Cook Time: 25-26 Min | Serves: 4

Calories: 154 | Fat: 3.1g | Carbs: 7.1g | Protein: 4.2g

INGREDIENTS

- 750g green beans
- Salt & black pepper
- 250g shallots, chopped
- 50g almonds, toasted
- 2 tbsp olive oil

DIRECTIONS

1. Trim and steam the green beans for 2 minutes.
2. Toss green beans with salt, pepper, shallots, almonds, and oil in the basket of your air fryer.
3. Cook for 25-26 Minutes at 205°C.
4. Serve and enjoy!

Creamy Air Fried Potato with Bacon Strips

Prep Time: 10-11 Min | Cook Time: 1 Hr 20 Min | Serves: 2

Calories: 175 | Fat: 5.1g | Carbs: 9.1g | Protein: 4.2g

INGREDIENTS

- 1 big potato
- 2 bacon strips
- 1 tsp olive oil
- 60g cheddar cheese, shredded
- 1 tbsp green onions, chopped
- Salt & black pepper
- 1 tbsp butter
- 2 tbsp heavy cream

DIRECTIONS

1. Cook and chop the bacon strips. Place potato in preheated air fryer and cook for 30-32 Minutes at 205°C after rubbing with oil and seasoning with salt and pepper.

2. Turn the potato over, cook it for an additional 30-32 Minutes, transfer it to a cutting board, let it cool, cut it in half lengthwise, and scrape the pulp into a bowl.

3. Fill potato skins with this mixture after thoroughly stirring in the bacon, cheese, butter, heavy cream, green onions, salt, and pepper.

4. Add the potatoes back to the air fryer and cook them for 20-21 Minutes at 205°C.

Roasted Pumpkin

Prep Time: 10-11 Min | Cook Time: 12-13 Min | Serves: 4

Calories: 201 | Fat: 5.1g | Carbs: 7.1g | Protein: 4.3g

INGREDIENTS

- 750g pumpkin
- 3 garlic cloves, minced
- 1 tbsp olive oil
- A pinch of sea salt
- A pinch of brown sugar
- A pinch of nutmeg, ground
- A pinch of cinnamon powder

DIRECTIONS

1. Deseed, slice and roughly chop the pumpkin.
2. Combine pumpkin with garlic, oil, salt, brown sugar, cinnamon, and nutmeg in the basket of your air fryer. Toss well. Cover.
3. Cook at 185°C for 12-13 Minutes.
4. Serve and enjoy!

Parmesan Mushrooms

Prep Time: 10-11 Min | Cook Time: 15-16 Min | Serves: 3

Calories: 122 | Fat: 4.1g | Carbs: 7.1g | Protein: 3.3g

INGREDIENTS

- 9 button mushroom caps
- 3 cream cracker slices, crumbled
- 1 egg white
- 2 tbsp parmesan, grated
- 1 tsp Italian seasoning
- Salt & black pepper
- 1 tbsp butter, melted

DIRECTIONS

1. To stuff mushrooms, combine crackers, egg white, parmesan, Italian seasoning, butter, salt, and pepper in a bowl. Stir well.

2. Arrange mushrooms in the basket of your air fryer and fry them for 15-16 Minutes at 180°C.

3. Serve and enjoy!

Stuffed Eggplant Lunch

Prep Time: 10-11 Min | Cook Time: 10-11 Min | Serves: 4

Calories: 203 | Fat: 3.1g | Carbs: 12.1g | Protein: 4.3g

INGREDIENTS

- 8 baby eggplants
- Salt & black pepper
- A pinch of oregano, dried
- 1 green bell pepper, chopped
- 1 tbsp tomato paste
- 1 bunch coriander, chopped
- ½ tsp garlic powder
- 1 tbsp olive oil
- 1 yellow onion, chopped
- 1 tomato chopped

DIRECTIONS

1. Scoop the eggplants and reserve the pulp. Add the onion to a skillet that has been heated with the oil over medium heat, stir, and cook for 1 minute.

2. Stir in the tomato, tomato paste, garlic powder, coriander, oregano, green bell pepper, salt, and pepper. Remove from heat. Let cool.

3. Stuff eggplants with this mixture, put them in the basket of your air fryer, and cook for 8 minutes at 180°C.

4. Distribute the eggplants among serving plates.

Pork Sausage with Rice

Prep Time: 10-11 Min | Cook Time: 20-21 Min | Serves: 4

Calories: 236 | Fat: 12.2g | Carbs: 20.1g | Protein: 13.5g

INGREDIENTS

- 400g white rice
- 1 tbsp butter
- Salt & black pepper
- 4 garlic cloves, minced
- 1 pork sausage, chopped
- 2 tbsp carrot, chopped
- 3 tbsp cheddar cheese, grated
- 2 tbsp mozzarella cheese, shredded

DIRECTIONS

1. Boil the white rice as per your preference. Preheat your air fryer at 175°C, add the butter, melt it, then add the garlic. Stir for two minutes.

2. Stir in the rice, carrots, sausage, salt, and pepper; then, bake for 10-11 Minutes at 175°C.

3. Stir in the cheese and serve by dividing into plates.

Cauliflower Cakes

Prep Time: 10-11 Min | Cook Time: 10-11 Min | Serves: 6

Calories: 124 | Fat: 2.1g | Carbs: 8.2g | Protein: 3.2g

INGREDIENTS

- 600g cauliflower rice
- 2 eggs
- 50g white flour
- 100g parmesan, grated
- Salt & black pepper
- Cooking spray

DIRECTIONS

1. Cauliflower rice should be combined with salt, pepper, and extra water in a bowl.

2. Transfer the cauliflower to a different bowl, combine the eggs, flour, parmesan, salt, and pepper, and whisk well before forming your cakes.

3. Spray cooking spray on your air fryer, preheat it to 205°C, add the cauliflower cakes, and cook them for 10-11 Minutes while flipping them halfway through.

4. Distribute cakes into serving dishes and serve.

Mushrooms with Bacon and Sour Cream

Prep Time: 10-11 Min | Cook Time: 10-11 Min | Serves: 6

Calories: 210 | Fat: 4.1g | Carbs: 8.1g | Protein: 3.1g

INGREDIENTS

- 2 bacon strips, chopped
- 1 yellow onion, chopped
- 1 green bell pepper, chopped
- 24 mushrooms
- 1 carrot, grated
- 125ml sour cream
- 100g cheddar cheese, grated
- Salt & black pepper

DIRECTIONS

1. Preheat a skillet over medium-high heat. Add the bacon, onion, bell pepper, and carrot. Stir and cook for one minute.

2. Add the sour cream, salt, and pepper, and stir. Cook for an additional minute, then turn off the heat.

3. Stuff mushrooms with this mixture, top with cheese, and cook for 8 minutes at 180°C.

4. Distribute among plates, then serve.

Creamy Brussels Sprouts

Prep Time: 10-11 Min | Cook Time: 25-26 Min | Serves: 8

Calories: 212 | Fat: 5.1g | Carbs: 11.9g | Protein: 5.2g

INGREDIENTS

- 1 ½ kg Brussels sprouts
- A drizzle of olive oil
- ½ kg bacon, chopped
- Salt & black pepper
- 4 tbsp butter
- 3 shallots, chopped
- 250ml milk
- 500ml heavy cream
- ¼ tsp nutmeg, ground
- 3 tbsp prepared horseradish

DIRECTIONS

1. With your air fryer preheated to 185°C, add the oil, bacon, salt, and pepper, followed by the Brussels sprouts, and toss.

2. Re-toss the mixture, then add the butter, shallots, heavy cream, milk, nutmeg, and horseradish. Cook for 25-26 Minutes.

3. Distribute across plates and serve.

Barley Risotto

Prep Time: 10-11 Min | Cook Time: 30-32 Min | Serves: 8

Calories: 122 | Fat: 4.1g | Carbs: 6.3g | Protein: 4.2g

INGREDIENTS

- 600ml veggie stock
- 3 tbsp olive oil
- 2 yellow onions, chopped
- 2 garlic cloves, minced
- 350g barley
- 85g mushrooms, sliced
- 60ml skim milk
- 1 tsp thyme, dried
- 1 tsp tarragon, dried
- Salt & black pepper
- 1 kg sweet potato

DIRECTIONS

1. Add barley to liquid in a pot, stir, and simmer for 15-16 Minutes over medium heat.

2. Heat the oil in your air fryer at 175°C.

3. Peel and chop the sweet potato. Stir in the sweet potato, barley, onions, garlic, mushrooms, milk, salt, and pepper. Cook for an additional 15-16 Minutes.

4. Distribute among plates, then serve.

Cauliflower Rice with Mushrooms

Prep Time: 10-11 Min | Cook Time: 40-42 Min | Serves: 8

Calories: 139 | Fat: 3.1g | Carbs: 6.2g | Protein: 4.4g

INGREDIENTS

- 1 tbsp peanut oil
- 1 tbsp sesame oil
- 4 tbsp soy sauce
- 3 garlic cloves, minced
- 1 tbsp ginger, grated
- Juice from ½ lemon
- 1 cauliflower head, riced
- 250g water chestnuts
- 150g peas
- 425g mushrooms, chopped
- 1 egg, whisked

DIRECTIONS

1. Cauliflower rice should be combined with peanut, sesame, soy, ginger, garlic, and lemon juice before being cooked in the air fryer for 20-21 Minutes at 175°C.

2. Stir in the chestnuts, peas, mushrooms, and egg. Cook at 180°C for an additional 20-21 Minutes.

3. Distribute among plates, then serve.

Beer Risotto

Prep Time: 10-11 Min | Cook Time: 30-32 Min | Serves: 4

Calories: 144 | Fat: 4.1g | Carbs: 6.1g | Protein: 4.2g

INGREDIENTS

- 2 tbsp olive oil
- 2 yellow onions, chopped
- 200g mushrooms, sliced
- 1 tsp basil, dried
- 1 tsp oregano, dried
- 300g rice
- 500ml beer
- 500ml chicken stock
- 1 tbsp butter
- 100g parmesan, grated

DIRECTIONS

1. Combine oil with onions, mushrooms, basil, and oregano in a dish that will fit in your air fryer and stir.

2. Place the rice, beer, butter, stock, and butter in the basket of your air fryer and cook for 30-32 Minutes at 175°C.

3. Distribute among dishes and sprinkle with freshly grated parmesan.

DINNER RECIPES

Thyme and Parsley Salmon

Prep Time: 10-11 Min | Cook Time: 15-16 Min | Serves: 4

Calories: 240 | Fat: 9.1g | Carbs: 20.4g | Protein: 30.8g

INGREDIENTS

- 4 salmon fillets, boneless
- Juice from 1 lemon
- 1 yellow onion, chopped
- 3 tomatoes, sliced
- 4 thyme springs
- 4 parsley springs
- 3 tbsp extra virgin olive oil
- Salt & black pepper

DIRECTIONS

1. In a pan that will fit your air fryer, drizzle 1 tbsp of oil, layer tomatoes on top, season with salt and pepper, drizzle 1 more tbsp of oil, add fish, season with salt and pepper, drizzle the remaining oil, top with thyme and parsley springs, onions, lemon juice, salt, and pepper, and place in the basket of your air fryer.

2. Cook at 180°C for 12-13 Minutes while shaking the pan occasionally.

3. Distribute everything among plates, then serve immediately.

Easy Duck Breasts

Prep Time: 10-11 Min | Cook Time: 40-42 Min | Serves: 4

Calories: 318 | Fat: 27.4g | Carbs: 12.1g | Protein: 41.7g

INGREDIENTS

- 6 duck breasts, halved
- Salt & black pepper
- 3 tbsp flour
- 6 tbsp butter, melted
- 400ml chicken stock
- 125ml white wine
- 50g parsley, chopped
- 400g mushrooms, chopped

DIRECTIONS

1. Place the duck breasts in a bowl, add the melted butter, stir, and transfer to an other bowl.

2. Gently whisk together the flour, wine, salt, pepper, and chicken stock with the melted butter.

3. Put the duck breasts in a baking dish that fits your air fryer, cover them with sauce, top with parsley, add mushrooms, and cook for 40-42 Minutes at 175°C.

4. Distribute among plates, then serve.

Garlic and Bell Pepper Beef

Prep Time: 30-32 Min | Cook Time: 30-32 Min | Serves: 4

Calories: 341 | Fat: 3.1g | Carbs: 26.2g | Protein: 37.3g

INGREDIENTS

- 300g steak fillets, sliced
- 4 garlic cloves, minced
- 2 tbsp olive oil
- 1 red bell pepper
- Black pepper to the taste
- 1 tbsp sugar
- 2 tbsp fish sauce
- 2 tsp corn flour
- 125ml beef stock
- 4 green onions, sliced

DIRECTIONS

1. Combine the beef with the oil, garlic, black pepper, and bell pepper (cut into strips) in a pan that will fit your air fryer. Stir, cover, and chill for 30-32 Minutes.

2. Place the pan in your prepared air fryer, and cook for 14 minutes at 180°C.

3. Combine sugar and fish sauce in a bowl, stir well, pour over beef, and simmer at 180°C for an additional 7 minutes.

4. Add the green onions, stock, and corn flour mixture, combine, and simmer for an additional 7 minutes at 185°C.

5. Arrange everything on plates and serve.

Spinach Pie

Prep Time: 10-11 Min | Cook Time: 15-16 Min | Serves: 4

Calories: 255 | Fat: 12.1g | Carbs: 23.3g | Protein: 12.3g

INGREDIENTS

- 200g flour
- 2 tbsp butter
- 200g spinach
- 1 tbsp olive oil
- 2 eggs
- 2 tbsp milk
- 85g cottage cheese
- Salt & black pepper
- 1 yellow onion, chopped

DIRECTIONS

1. In a food processor, combine the flour, butter, milk, salt, and pepper; process until well combined; transfer to a bowl; knead; cover; and let sit for 10-11 Minutes.

2. Add the onion and spinach to a pan that has been heated with the oil over medium-high heat, stir, and cook for 2 minutes.

3. Stir well, then turn the heat off after adding salt, pepper, the remaining egg, and cottage cheese.

4. Divide the dough into 4 equal pieces, roll each piece, and lay it on the bottom of a ramekin. Next, top the dough with the spinach filling. Put the ramekins in the basket of your air fryer and cook for 15-16 Minutes at 180°C.

5. Serve hot.

Trout with Butter Sauce

Prep Time: 10-11 Min | Cook Time: 10-11 Min | Serves: 4

Calories: 304 | Fat: 12.1g | Carbs: 26.4g | Protein: 23.9g

INGREDIENTS

- 4 trout fillets, boneless
- Salt & black pepper
- 3 tsp lemon zest, grated
- 3 tbsp chives, chopped
- 6 tbsp butter
- 2 tbsp olive oil
- 2 tsp lemon juice

DIRECTIONS

1. Rub the fish with salt and pepper, sprinkle it with olive oil, and then move it to your air fryer. Cook it for 10-11 Minutes at 180°C, flipping it once.

2. In the meantime, melt the butter in a medium-sized saucepan. Add the chives, lemon juice, and zest. Whisk to combine. Cook for 1 to 2 minutes, then turn off the heat.

3. Distribute the fish fillets among plates, top with butter sauce, and serve.

Duck Breasts with Endives

Prep Time: 10-11 Min | Cook Time: 25-26 Min | Serves: 4

Calories: 402 | Fat: 12.4g | Carbs: 28.1g | Protein: 27.9g

INGREDIENTS

- 2 duck breasts
- Salt & black pepper
- 1 tbsp sugar
- 1 tbsp olive oil
- 6 endives, julienned
- 2 tbsp cranberries
- 235ml white wine
- 1 tbsp garlic, minced
- 2 tbsp heavy cream

DIRECTIONS

1. Duck breasts that have been scored and season with salt and pepper should be cooked at 175°C for 20-21 Minutes, flipping them halfway through

2. In the meantime, preheat a medium-sized skillet with the oil, add the sugar, and sauté the endives for 2 minutes, stirring occasionally.

3. Stir in the cranberries, wine, cream, salt, and pepper. Cook for 3 minutes.

4. Distribute the duck breasts among plates, top with the endives sauce, and serve.

Marinated Lamb and Veggies

Prep Time: 10-11 Min | Cook Time: 30-32 Min | Serves: 4

Calories: 268 | Fat: 3.1g | Carbs: 18.4g | Protein: 22.3g

INGREDIENTS

- 1 carrot, chopped
- 1 onion, sliced
- ½ tbsp olive oil
- 85g bean sprouts
- 225g lamb loin, sliced

For the marinade:

- 1 garlic clove, minced
- ½ apple, grated
- Salt & black pepper
- 1 small yellow onion, grated
- 1 tbsp ginger, grated
- 5 tbsp soy sauce
- 1 tbsp sugar
- 2 tbsp orange juice

DIRECTIONS

1. Add the grated onion, apple, garlic, ginger, soy sauce, orange juice, sugar, and black pepper to a bowl and whisk to combine. Add the lamb and set aside for 10-11 Minutes.

2. Add one sliced onion, one carrot, and bean sprouts to an air fryer-compatible pan that has been heated with olive oil over medium-high heat. Stir and cook for three minutes.

3. Place the pan in the preheated air fryer, add the lamb, and cook for 25-26 Minutes at 180°C.

4. Serve in bowls and enjoy!

Balsamic Artichokes

Prep Time: 10-11 Min | Cook Time: 7 Min | Serves: 4

Calories: 203 | Fat: 3.1g | Carbs: 12.3g | Protein: 4.3g

INGREDIENTS

- 4 big artichokes, trimmed
- Salt & black pepper
- 2 tbsp lemon juice
- 50ml extra-virgin olive oil
- 2 tsp balsamic vinegar
- 1 tsp oregano, dried
- 2 garlic cloves, minced

DIRECTIONS

1. Rub the artichokes with half the oil and half the lemon juice after seasoning them with salt and pepper. Place the artichokes in your air fryer and cook for 7 minutes at 180°C.

2. In the meantime, thoroughly combine the remaining lemon juice, vinegar, remaining oil, salt, pepper, garlic, and oregano in a bowl.

3. Arrange the artichokes on a dish and top them with the balsamic vinaigrette before serving.

Creamy Salmon

Prep Time: 10-11 Min | Cook Time: 10-11 Min | Serves: 4

Calories: 201 | Fat: 6.1g | Carbs: 17.2g | Protein: 20.3g

INGREDIENTS

- 4 salmon fillets, boneless
- 1 tbsp olive oil
- Salt & black pepper
- 150g cheddar cheese, grated
- 1 and ½ tsp mustard
- 125ml coconut cream

DIRECTIONS

1. Rub salmon generously with salt and pepper before adding the oil.

2. Combine coconut cream, cheddar, mustard, salt, and pepper in a bowl and toss to combine.

3. Insert a pan that will fit your air fryer, pour the coconut cream mixture, and cook the salmon for 10-11 Minutes at 160°C.

4. Distribute among plates, then serve.

Chicken Breasts with Tomatoes Sauce

Prep Time: 10-11 Min | Cook Time: 20-21 Min | Serves: 4

Calories: 255 | Fat: 12.1g | Carbs: 19.2g | Protein: 28.4g

INGREDIENTS

- 1 red onion, chopped
- 4 chicken breasts
- 60ml balsamic vinegar
- 400g canned tomatoes, chopped
- Salt & black pepper
- 50g parmesan, grated
- ¼ tsp garlic powder
- Cooking spray

DIRECTIONS

1. Place the chicken in a baking dish that fits your air fryer, season with salt, pepper, balsamic vinegar, garlic powder, tomatoes, and cheese, stir, and cook for 20-21 Minutes at 205°C.

2. Distribute among plates, then warmly serve.

Creamy Lamb

Prep Time: 24 Hr | Cook Time: 60 Min | Serves: 8

Calories: 288 | Fat: 4.1g | Carbs: 19.7g | Protein: 25.1g

INGREDIENTS

- 2 ½ kg leg of lamb
- 400ml low fat buttermilk
- 2 tbsp mustard
- 100g butter
- 2 tbsp basil, chopped
- 2 tbsp tomato paste
- 2 garlic cloves, minced
- Salt & black pepper
- 250ml white wine
- 1 tbsp cornstarch + 1 tbsp water
- 125ml sour cream

DIRECTIONS

1. Place the lamb roast in a large dish, cover it, add the buttermilk, and toss to coat. Refrigerate for 24 hours.

2. Dry off the lamb and place it in a pan designed for your air fryer.

3. Spread the butter mixture over the lamb in a dish along with the tomato paste, mustard, basil, rosemary, salt, pepper, and garlic. Place the bowl in the air fryer and cook the lamb for an hour at 150°C.

4. Slice the lamb, divide it among plates, and set it aside while you reheat the cooking liquids in the stovetop pan.

5. Pour this sauce over the lamb before serving and add the wine, cornstarch mixture, salt, pepper, and sour cream while stirring.

Cheesy Artichokes

Prep Time: 10-11 Min | Cook Time: 6 Min | Serves: 6

Calories: 260 | Fat: 12.1g | Carbs: 12.3g | Protein: 15.3g

INGREDIENTS

- 400g canned artichoke hearts
- 220ml cream cheese
- 450g parmesan cheese, grated
- 250g spinach
- 125ml chicken stock
- 225g mozzarella, shredded
- 125ml sour cream
- 3 garlic cloves, minced
- 125ml mayonnaise
- 1 tsp onion powder

DIRECTIONS

1. Toss artichokes with stock, garlic, spinach, cream cheese, sour cream, onion powder, and mayonnaise in a pan that will fit your air fryer. Place the pan in your air fryer and cook for 6 minutes at 175°C.

2. After thoroughly stirring, add the mozzarella and parmesan.

Italian Barramundi Fillets and Tomato Salsa

Prep Time: 10-11 Min | Cook Time: 8 Min | Serves: 4

Calories: 274 | Fat: 4.1g | Carbs: 18.1g | Protein: 26.4g

INGREDIENTS

- 2 barramundi fillets, boneless
- 1 tbsp olive oil+ 2 tsp
- 2 tsp Italian seasoning
- 50g green olives
- 50g cherry tomatoes, chopped
- 50g black olives, chopped
- 1 tbsp lemon zest
- 2 tbsp lemon zest
- Salt & black pepper
- 2 tbsp parsley, chopped

DIRECTIONS

1. Season the fish with salt, pepper, Italian seasoning, and 2 tbsp of extra virgin olive oil. Transfer to your air fryer and cook for 8 minutes at 180°C, flipping the fish halfway through.

2. Combine tomatoes, black olives (pitted and chopped), green olives, salt, pepper, lemon juice and zest, parsley, and 1 tbsp olive oil in a bowl and toss to combine.

3. Distribute the fish among plates, top with the tomato salsa, and serve.

Chicken and Asparagus

Prep Time: 10-11 Min | Cook Time: 20-21 Min | Serves: 4

Calories: 268 | Fat: 8.1g | Carbs: 24.2g | Protein: 22.3g

INGREDIENTS

- 8 chicken wings, halved
- 8 asparagus spears
- Salt & black pepper
- 1 tbsp rosemary, chopped
- 1 tsp cumin, ground

DIRECTIONS

1. Dry off the chicken wings, season with salt, pepper, cumin, and rosemary, place them in the basket of your air fryer, and cook for 20-21 Minutes at 180°C.

2. In the meantime, preheat a medium-sized skillet, add the asparagus, cover with water, and steam for a few minutes. Transfer the asparagus to a bowl of ice water, drain it, and arrange it on plates.

3. Finish by serving with chicken wings on the side.

Lamb Shanks

Prep Time: 10-11 Min | Cook Time: 45 Min | Serves: 4

Calories: 285 | Fat: 4.1g | Carbs: 17.2g | Protein: 26.3g

INGREDIENTS

- 4 lamb shanks
- 1 yellow onion, chopped
- 1 tbsp olive oil
- 4 tsp coriander seeds, crushed
- 2 tbsp white flour
- 4 bay leaves
- 2 tsp honey
- 150ml dry sherry
- 500ml chicken stock
- Salt & pepper

DIRECTIONS

1. Rub half of the oil over the lamb shanks before seasoning with salt and pepper. Place in the air fryer and cook for 10-11 Minutes at 180°C.

2. Add the onion and coriander to the remaining oil that has been heated in a pan that fits your air fryer, swirl, and cook for 5 minutes.

3. Combine everything in your air fryer and cook at 180°C for 30-32 Minutes. Add the lamb after stirring in the flour, sherry, stock, honey, and bay leaves.

4. Serve on plates and enjoy!

Beet Salad and Parsley Dressing

Prep Time: 10-11 Min | Cook Time: 14 Min | Serves: 4

Calories: 72 | Fat: 2.1g | Carbs: 6.3g | Protein: 4.1g

INGREDIENTS

- 4 beets
- 2 tbsp balsamic vinegar
- A bunch of parsley, chopped
- Salt & black pepper
- 1 tbsp extra virgin olive oil
- 1 garlic clove, chopped
- 2 tbsp capers

DIRECTIONS

1. Cook beets in your air fryer for 14 minutes at 180°C.

2. In the meantime, thoroughly combine the parsley, garlic, salt, pepper, olive oil, and capers in a bowl.

3. Place the beets on a chopping board, let them cool, then slice, peel, and place them in a salad bowl.

4. Stir in the vinegar, then top with the parsley dressing and serve.

Salmon with Avocado Salsa

Prep Time: 30-32 Min | Cook Time: 10-11 Min | Serves: 4

Calories: 303 | Fat: 14.1g | Carbs: 18.2g | Protein: 16.1g

INGREDIENTS

- 4 salmon fillets
- 1 tbsp olive oil
- Salt & black pepper
- 1 tsp cumin, ground
- 1 tsp sweet paprika
- ½ tsp chili powder
- 1 tsp garlic powder

For the salsa:

- 1 small red onion, chopped
- 1 avocado
- 2 tbsp cilantro, chopped
- Juice from 2 limes
- Salt & black pepper

DIRECTIONS

1. Combine salt, pepper, chili powder, onion powder, paprika, and cumin in a bowl; stir. Rub this mixture all over the salmon; sprinkle with oil; rub again; transfer to an air fryer; and cook for 5 minutes on each side at 175°C.

2. In the meantime, combine avocado (pitted, peeled and chopped) with red onion, salt, pepper, cilantro, and lime juice in a bowl and toss to combine.

3. Arrange fillets on plates, add avocado salsa over top, and then serve.

Chicken Thighs and Apple Mix

Prep Time: 12 Hr | Cook Time: 30-32 Min | Serves: 4

Calories: 315 | Fat: 8.1g | Carbs: 34.7g | Protein: 22.5g

INGREDIENTS

- 8 chicken thighs
- Salt & black pepper
- 1 tbsp apple cider vinegar
- 3 tbsp onion, chopped
- 1 tbsp ginger, grated
- ½ tsp thyme, dried
- 3 apples
- 150ml apple juice
- 125ml maple syrup

DIRECTIONS

1. Combine the chicken in a bowl with the apple juice, maple syrup, onion, ginger, salt, and pepper. Toss well, cover, and refrigerate for 12 hours.

2. Place the entire mixture in a baking dish that will fit your air fryer, top with apple slices (remove the core and cut into quarters), and cook for 30-32 Minutes at 175°C.

3. Distribute among plates, then warmly serve.

Lamb Roast with Potatoes

Prep Time: 10-11 Min | Cook Time: 45 Min | Serves: 6

Calories: 277 | Fat: 4.1g | Carbs: 25.3g | Protein: 29.3g

INGREDIENTS

- 2 kg lamb roast
- 1 spring rosemary
- 3 garlic cloves, minced
- 6 potatoes, halved
- 125ml lamb stock
- 4 bay leaves
- Salt & black pepper

DIRECTIONS

1. Place the potatoes in the air fryer-compatible dish, add the lamb, garlic, rosemary sprigs, salt, pepper, bay leaves, and stock, stir, and cook for 45 minutes at 180°C.

2. Slice the lamb and serve it with the potatoes and cooking liquids on individual plates.

Artichokes and Special Sauce

Prep Time: 10-11 Min | Cook Time: 6 Min | Serves: 2

Calories: 266 | Fat: 4.1g | Carbs: 20.3g | Protein: 12.3g

INGREDIENTS

- 2 artichokes, trimmed
- A drizzle of olive oil
- 2 garlic cloves, minced
- 1 tbsp lemon juice

For the sauce:

- 50ml coconut oil
- 50ml extra virgin olive oil
- 3 anchovy fillets
- 3 garlic cloves

DIRECTIONS

1. Toss the artichokes with the oil, lemon juice, and 2 garlic cloves in a bowl. Transfer to the air fryer and cook at 175°C for 6 minutes before dividing among plates.

2. Combine coconut oil, anchovies, three garlic cloves, and olive oil in a food processor and pulse until very smooth. Drizzle mixture over artichokes and serve.

SNACKS RECIPES

Wrapped Shrimp

Prep Time: 10-11 Min | Cook Time: 8 Min | Serves: 16

Calories: 225 | Fat: 12.1g | Carbs: 12.3g | Protein: 14.1g

INGREDIENTS

- 2 tbsp olive oil
- 285g shrimps
- 1 tbsp mint, chopped
- 150g blackberries, ground
- 11 prosciutto, sliced
- 150ml red wine

DIRECTIONS

1. Place each shrimp (already cooked, peeled and deveined) in a prosciutto slice before adding oil and giving them a good rub. Set your air fryer to 200°C and fried the shrimp for 8 minutes.

2. In the meantime, preheat a medium-sized skillet with ground blackberries, add mint and wine, swirl, cook for 3 minutes, and then turn off the heat.

3. Arrange shrimp on a dish, top with a sauce made from blackberries, and serve as a snack.

Broccoli Patties

Prep Time: 10-11 Min | Cook Time: 10-11 Min | Serves: 12

Calories: 205 | Fat: 12.1g | Carbs: 14.3g | Protein: 2.1g

INGREDIENTS

- 800g broccoli florets
- 350g almond flour
- 1 tsp paprika
- Salt & black pepper
- 2 eggs
- 50ml olive oil
- 400g cheddar cheese, grated
- 1 tsp garlic powder
- ½ tsp apple cider vinegar
- ½ tsp baking soda

DIRECTIONS

1. Place the broccoli florets in the food processor, season with salt and pepper, and pulse until well combined.

2. Combine the ingredients thoroughly, then add the almond flour, salt, pepper, paprika, garlic powder, baking soda, cheese, oil, eggs, and vinegar. Form 12 patties from this mixture.

3. Put them in the basket of your preheated air fryer, and cook for 10-11 Minutes at 175°C.

4. Arrange the patties on a tray and serve them as a snack.

Meat & Cheese Stuffed Peppers

Prep Time: 10-11 Min | Cook Time: 20-21 Min | Serves: 6

Calories: 174 | Fat: 22.1g | Carbs: 6.3g | Protein: 27.1g

INGREDIENTS

- ½ kg mini bell peppers, halved
- Salt & black pepper
- 1 tsp garlic powder
- 1 tsp sweet paprika
- ½ tsp oregano, dried
- ¼ tsp red pepper flakes
- ½ kg beef meat, ground
- 300g cheddar cheese, shredded
- 1 tbsp chili powder
- 1 tsp cumin, ground
- Sour cream for serving

DIRECTIONS

1. Stir the following ingredients into the chili powder: paprika, salt, pepper, cumin, oregano, pepper flakes, and garlic powder.

2. In a skillet that has been heated to medium heat, add the meat, stir, and brown it for 10-11 Minutes.

3. Add the chili powder mixture, stir, turn off the heat, and put the mixture into the pepper halves.

4. Top the peppers with cheese and cook them in the basket of your air fryer for 6 minutes at 175°C.

5. Arrange the peppers on a serving plate and add sour cream to the side.

Cheesy Zucchini Snack

Prep Time: 10-11 Min | Cook Time: 8 Min | Serves: 4

Calories: 154 | Fat: 4.1g | Carbs: 12.3g | Protein: 4.1g

INGREDIENTS

- 200g mozzarella, shredded
- 75ml tomato sauce
- 1 zucchini, sliced
- Salt & black pepper
- A pinch of cumin
- Cooking spray

DIRECTIONS

1. Arrange the zucchini slices in the basket of your air fryer, spray them with cooking oil, cover them with tomato sauce, season with salt, pepper, and cumin, top with mozzarella, and cook for 8 minutes at 160°C.

2. Place them on a tray and serve them as a snack.

Spinach Balls

Prep Time: 10-11 Min | Cook Time: 7 Min | Serves: 30

Calories: 63 | Fat: 5.1g | Carbs: 1.3g | Protein: 2.1g

INGREDIENTS

- 4 tbsp butter, melted
- 2 eggs
- 200g flour
- 450g spinach
- 150g feta cheese, crumbled
- ¼ tsp nutmeg, ground
- 150g parmesan, grated
- Salt & black pepper
- 1 tbsp onion powder
- 3 tbsp whipping cream
- 1 tsp garlic powder

DIRECTIONS

1. Blend spinach very well in your blender with the butter, eggs, flour, feta cheese, parmesan, nutmeg, whipped cream, salt, pepper, onion, and garlic powder. Place in freezer for 10-11 Minutes.

2. Form 30 spinach balls, put them in the basket of your air fryer, and cook for 7 minutes at 150°C.

3. Use as a snack. Enjoy!

Mayo Mushrooms Snack

Prep Time: 10-11 Min | Cook Time: 10-11 Min | Serves: 4

Calories: 63 | Fat: 5.1g | Carbs: 1.3g | Protein: 2.1g

INGREDIENTS

- 60ml mayonnaise
- 1 tsp garlic powder
- 1 small yellow onion, chopped
- 650g white mushroom caps
- Salt & black pepper
- 1 tsp curry powder
- 120ml cream cheese
- 150ml sour cream
- 100g Mexican cheese, shredded
- 250g shrimp

DIRECTIONS

1. Cook, peel, devein and chop the shrimps.

2. Combine mayonnaise, shrimp, cream cheese, sour cream, Mexican cheese, garlic powder, onion, curry powder, and salt and pepper to taste in a bowl.

3. Stuff the mushrooms with this mixture, put them in the basket of your air fryer, and cook for 10-11 Minutes at 150°C.

4. Arrange and serve as a snack.

Cheesy Party Wings

Prep Time: 10-11 Min | Cook Time: 12-13 Min | Serves: 6

Calories: 205 | Fat: 8.1g | Carbs: 18.2g | Protein: 14.1g

INGREDIENTS

- 3 kg chicken wings
- Salt & black pepper
- ½ tsp Italian seasoning
- 2 tbsp butter
- 100g parmesan cheese, grated
- Red pepper flakes
- 1 tsp garlic powder
- 1 egg

DIRECTIONS

1. Arrange chicken wings in the basket of your air fryer, and cook for 9 minutes at 200°C.

2. In the meantime, combine the butter, cheese, egg, salt, pepper, pepper flakes, garlic powder, and Italian seasoning in your blender and process until extremely smooth.

3. Remove the chicken wings from the air fryer basket, cover them with cheese sauce, toss to evenly coat, and cook for 3 minutes at 200°C.

4. Serve and enjoy!

Sweet Bacon Snack

Prep Time: 10-11 Min | Cook Time: 30-32 Min | Serves: 6

Calories: 204 | Fat: 4.1g | Carbs: 12.2g | Protein: 3.1g

INGREDIENTS

- ½ tsp cinnamon powder
- 16 bacon slices
- 1 tbsp avocado oil
- 85g dark chocolate
- 1 tsp maple extract

DIRECTIONS

1. Arrange bacon slices in the basket of your air fryer, sprinkle cinnamon mixture over them, and cook for 30-32 Minutes at 150°C.

2. Melt the chocolate in a pot with the oil over medium heat by adding it and stirring constantly.

3. Stir in the maple extract, remove from heat, and set aside to cool somewhat.

4. Remove the bacon strips from the oven, let them cool, then dip each one in the chocolate mixture before laying them out on parchment paper to finish cooling.

5. Serve cold and enjoy!

Cheese Sticks

Prep Time: 1 Hr 10-11 Min | Cook Time: 8 Min | Serves: 16

Calories: 143 | Fat: 5.1g | Carbs: 3.2g | Protein: 4.1g

INGREDIENTS

- 2 eggs, whisked
- Salt & black pepper
- 8 mozzarella cheese strings
- 200g parmesan, grated
- 1 tbsp Italian seasoning
- Cooking spray
- 1 garlic clove, minced

DIRECTIONS

1. Combine the parmesan, garlic, Italian seasoning, salt, and pepper in a bowl and whisk well.

2. Add whipped eggs to a different bowl.

3. Afterward, dip mozzarella sticks in the cheese mixture.

4. After a second egg and parmesan mixture dip, freeze the items for an hour.

5. Cook cheese sticks in the basket of your air fryer at 200°C for 8 minutes, rotating them halfway through. Serve and enjoy!

Blue Cheese Chicken Rolls

Prep Time: 2 Hr 10-11 Min | Cook Time: 10-11 Min | Serves: 12

Calories: 219 | Fat: 7.1g | Carbs: 14.2g | Protein: 10.1g

INGREDIENTS

- 115g blue cheese, crumbled
- 500g chicken
- Salt & black pepper
- 2 green onions, chopped
- 2 celery stalks, chopped
- 100ml tomato sauce
- 12 egg roll wrappers
- Cooking spray

DIRECTIONS

1. Combine the chicken (cooked and chopped), blue cheese, salt, pepper, celery, green onions, and tomato sauce in a bowl. Stir thoroughly, then chill for 2 hours.

2. Lay egg wrappers out on a work surface, distribute the chicken mixture among them, and then roll and seal the edges.

3. Put the rolls in the basket of your air fryer, coat them with cooking oil, and cook them for 10-11 Minutes at 175°C, flipping them halfway through.

DESSERT RECIPES

Lemon Bars

Prep Time: 10-11 Min | Cook Time: 25-26 Min | Serves: 6

Calories: 128 | Fat: 4.1g | Carbs: 16.0g | Protein: 12.2g

INGREDIENTS

- 4 eggs
- 600g flour
- Juice from 2 lemons
- 200g butter, soft
- 200g sugar

DIRECTIONS

1. In a bowl, combine butter, 400g flour, and 100g sugar. Stir well. Press the mixture into the bottom of a pan designed for an air fryer. Cook for 10-11 Minutes at 175°C.

2. Combine the remaining sugar, remaining flour, remaining eggs, and lemon juice in a separate bowl. Whisk thoroughly and spread over crust.

3. Add to the fryer for 15 more minutes at 175°C, set aside to cool, then cut into bars and serve.

Pears with Espresso Cream

Prep Time: 10-11 Min | Cook Time: 30-32 Min | Serves: 4

Calories: 213 | Fat: 5.1g | Carbs: 8.2g | Protein: 7.2g

INGREDIENTS

- 4 pears, halved and cored
- 2 tbsp lemon juice
- 1 tbsp sugar
- 2 tbsp water
- 2 tbsp butter

For the cream:

- 250ml whipping cream
- 250ml mascarpone
- 140g sugar
- 2 tbsp espresso, cold

DIRECTIONS

1. Toss the pear halves with the butter, water, lemon juice, and 1 tbsp of sugar in a bowl. Then, add the mixture to the air fryer and cook for 30-32 Minutes at 180°C.

2. In the meantime, combine the whipped cream, mascarpone, sugar, and espresso in a bowl, whisk thoroughly, and chill until the pears are tender.

3. Distribute the pears among plates, then serve them with espresso cream on top.

Figs and Coconut Butter Mix

Prep Time: 6 Min | Cook Time: 4 Min | Serves: 3

Calories: 172 | Fat: 4.1g | Carbs: 7.2g | Protein: 9.1g

INGREDIENTS

- 2 tbsp coconut butter
- 12 figs, halved
- 50g sugar
- 200g almonds

DIRECTIONS

1. Melt the butter in an air fryer-compatible pan over medium-high heat.

2. Combine the figs, sugar, and almonds (toasted and chopped) in your air fryer. Cook for 4 minutes at 150°C.

3. Serve chilled in bowls.

Poppyseed Cake

Prep Time: 10-11 Min | Cook Time: 30-32 Min | Serves: 6

Calories: 214 | Fat: 6.1g | Carbs: 12.2g | Protein: 6.1g

INGREDIENTS

- 350g flour
- 1 tsp baking powder
- 140g sugar
- 1 tbsp orange zest, grated
- 2 tsp lime zest, grated
- 100g butter, soft
- 2 eggs, whisked
- ½ tsp vanilla extract
- 2 tbsp poppy seeds
- 250ml milk

For the cream:

- 200g sugar
- 100g passion fruit puree
- 3 tbsp butter, melted
- 4 egg yolks

DIRECTIONS

1. Combine the flour, baking powder, 50g sugar, orange zest, and lime zest in a bowl and stir to combine.

2. Pour the ingredients into an air fryer-compatible cake pan, stir with a mixer to combine, and bake at 175°C for about 30 minutes.

3. In the meantime, melt 3 tbsp of butter in a skillet over medium heat. When you've finished, add the sugar and mix to combine.

4. Turn off the heat and whisk vigorously before gradually adding the pureed passion fruit.

5. Remove the cake from the fryer, let it cool, and then cut it in half horizontally.

6. Top the cake with the second half and spread the remaining ¼ of the passion fruit cream on top. Serve cold and enjoy!

Sweet Squares

Prep Time: 10-11 Min | Cook Time: 30-32 Min | Serves: 6

Calories: 102 | Fat: 4.1g | Carbs: 12.1g | Protein: 1.1g

INGREDIENTS

- 250g flour
- 100g butter, soft
- 200g sugar
- 50g powdered sugar
- 2 tsp lemon peel, grated
- 2 tbsp lemon juice
- 2 eggs, whisked
- ½ tsp baking powder

DIRECTIONS

1. In a bowl, combine flour, powdered sugar, and butter; stir well. Press the mixture into the bottom of a pan that will fit inside your air fryer; place the pan into the fryer; and bake for 14 minutes at 175°C.

2. In a separate bowl, combine the sugar, eggs, baking powder, lemon juice, and lemon peel. Stir with a mixer, then spread the mixture over the cooked crust.

3. Bake for a further 15 minutes, then remove to cool completely before cutting into medium squares and serving cold.

Plum Bars

Prep Time: 10-11 Min | Cook Time: 16 Min | Serves: 8

Calories: 110 | Fat: 5.1g | Carbs: 12.1g | Protein: 6.2g

INGREDIENTS

- 400g dried plums
- 6 tbsp water
- 400g rolled oats
- 200g brown sugar
- ½ tsp baking soda
- 1 tsp cinnamon powder
- 2 tbsp butter, melted
- 1 egg, whisked
- Cooking spray

DIRECTIONS

1. To make a sticky spread, combine plums and water in your food processor and process until smooth.

2. Combine the oats, cinnamon, baking soda, sugar, egg, and butter in a bowl and stir well.

3. Press half of the oat mixture into an air fryer-compatible baking pan, pour the plum mixture over it, and then cover it with the remaining oat mixture.

4. Add the ingredients to your air fryer and cook for 16 minutes at 175°C.

5. Let the mixture cool before cutting it into medium bars and serving.

Orange Cookies

Prep Time: 10-11 Min | Cook Time: 12-13 Min | Serves: 8

Calories: 125 | Fat: 5.1g | Carbs: 8.1g | Protein: 4.2g

INGREDIENTS

- 500g flour
- 1 tsp baking powder
- 100g butter, soft
- 150g sugar
- 1 egg, whisked
- 1 tsp vanilla extract
- 1 tbsp orange zest, grated

For the filling:

- 100ml cream cheese, soft
- 100g butter
- 300g powdered sugar

DIRECTIONS

1. Combine the cream cheese, 100g butter, and 300g powdered sugar in a bowl. Beat well with an electric mixer and set aside for the time being.

2. Combine the flour and baking powder in a separate basin.

3. In a third dish, whisk together 100g butter, 150g sugar, an egg, vanilla essence, and orange zest.

4. Mix the flour and orange mixture thoroughly, then put 1 spoonful of the mixture onto a prepared baking sheet that is large enough to suit your air fryer.

5. Repeat with the remaining orange batter, add to the fryer, and cook for 12 minutes at 170°C.

6. After the cookies have cooled, spread half of them with cream filling, top them with the remaining cookies, and serve.

Plum and Currant Tart

Prep Time: 30-32 Min | Cook Time: 35 Min | Serves: 6

Calories: 203 | Fat: 5.1g | Carbs: 8.1g | Protein: 6.3g

INGREDIENTS

For the crumble:

- 50g almond flour
- 50g millet flour
- 200g brown rice flour
- 100g cane sugar
- 10 tbsp butter, soft
- 3 tbsp milk

For the filling:

- ½ kg small plums
- 200g white currants
- 2 tbsp cornstarch
- 3 tbsp sugar
- ½ tsp vanilla extract
- ½ tsp cinnamon powder
- ¼ tsp ginger powder
- 1 tsp lime juice

DIRECTIONS

1. To create a dough that resembles sand, combine brown rice flour, 100g sugar, millet flour, almond flour, butter, and milk in a bowl.

2. Set aside ¼ of the dough and push the remaining dough into an air fryer-compatible tart pan. Refrigerate for 30 minutes.

3. In the meantime, combine the plums (pitted and halved), currants, 3 tbsp sugar, cornstarch, vanilla, cinnamon, ginger, and lime juice in a bowl and whisk to combine.

4. Pour this over the tart shell, sprinkle with the leftover dough, place in the air fryer, and cook for 35 minutes at 175°C.

5. Let tart cool before slicing and serving.

Cashew Bars

Prep Time: 10-11 Min | Cook Time: 15-16 Min | Serves: 6

Calories: 122 | Fat: 4.1g | Carbs: 5.2g | Protein: 5.9g

INGREDIENTS

- 150ml honey
- 50g almond meal
- 1 tbsp almond butter
- 300g cashews, chopped
- 4 dates, chopped
- 150g coconut, shredded
- 1 tbsp chia seeds

DIRECTIONS

1. Combine honey, almond butter, and almond meal in a bowl and whisk thoroughly.

2. Continue to thoroughly whisk in the cashews, coconut, dates, and chia seeds.

3. Distribute this evenly and firmly on a prepared baking sheet that will fit your air fryer.

4. Add to the fryer and cook for 15 minutes at 150°C.

5. Let the mixture cool before cutting it into medium bars to serve.

Brown Butter Cookies

Prep Time: 10-11 Min | Cook Time: 10-11 Min | Serves: 6

Calories: 147 | Fat: 5.1g | Carbs: 19.2g | Protein: 2.1g

INGREDIENTS

- 300g butter
- 350g brown sugar
- 2 eggs, whisked
- 750g flour
- 150g pecans, chopped
- 2 tsp vanilla extract
- 1 tsp baking soda
- ½ tsp baking powder

DIRECTIONS

1. Melt the butter in a pan over medium heat, add the brown sugar, and whisk until the sugar is dissolved.

2. Combine flour, pecans, vanilla extract, baking soda, baking powder, and eggs in a bowl and stir to combine.

3. Stir in the brown butter, then add spoonfuls of the mixture to a prepared baking sheet that is designed to suit your air fryer.

4. Add the food to the fryer and cook for 10 minutes at 170°C.

5. Allow cookies to cool before serving.

Printed in Great Britain
by Amazon